THE SINGERS
&
THE NOTES

DUSIE

A C K N O W L E D G M E N T S

Some parts of this book first appeared (in slightly different versions) in the following publications: *Drill, Matter, Hot Whiskey Magazine, Spell, string of small machines, the tiny, Bombay Gin,* & online at *Meloncholia's Tremulous Dreadlocks,* & *Turn Table & Blue Light.* My thanks to the editors of those publications.

I would like to thank Armand F. Capanna II, Michael Slosek, John Sakkis & Michael Koshkin for all the care & interest they've taken in my work. As well, I'd like to thank Larry Kearney, Kevin Killian, & Brandon Brown for their careful reading of *The Singers.* I'd also like to thank Susan Gardner for her generosity and enthusiasm for putting out this second edition of *The Singers,* which now includes *The Notes,* a natural extension of the first version of this book. And of course I'd like to thank all my friends and family.

Some lines in these books have been adapted or lifted from the following: Joy Division, Stacey Q, My Morning Jacket, Steve Orth/Shivshark, The Cure, Radiohead, R.E.M, Morrissey, Clouddead, The Smiths, Nitzer Ebb, Laura Branigan, The Smashing Pumpkins, David Bowie, TV on the Radio, Robert Palmer, The Faint, Bjork, Paul Simon, New Order, Bright Eyes, Modest Mouse, Front 242, Interpol, The Police, The Killers, Sufjan Stevens, Clap Your Hands Say Yeah!, Depeche Mode, Wire, WAH!, & the San Francisco Giants baseball radio announcers Jon Miller, Dave Flemming, Duane Kiper & Mike Krukow.

Logan Ryan Smith
San Francisco, 2009

ISBN: 978-0-6151-4235-7

Cover Design by the editor

Dusie books are published by Dusie Press,
Susana Gardner, ed,-

: Dusie Press : Zürich, Switzerland :
: editor@dusie.org : http://www.dusie.org :

THE SINGERS

You're whole life as an uncoordinated bridge-worker.

Supsension. Dis-.

Belief. Tongue. Under. Water.

> Under limbs hung of human flesh there is little control.
> Under limbs of skin and bone there is accident, often.

Gather together. Count and call
voices that sing, call them and sing them, sing this:
        Sing this: Sing, my hour the hour
the sky above my feet
are like glass,
        my life is almost
hourglass-sing,
a moment in imagination
    there's something
in limbs
in the reach of great birds and animals
something well-worth the wait for the drink
from the cup worth seeking

there's something there my God
there's something.

Sing   and wait   to be sung to.

Hear: grapevine growth. Creek water run. Crickets' legs break.

Gravity carries crickets over the field, over the song.
The song is long over, not gone, and barely sung.

Lights in the forest are calling for the dead.
They're singing to them, making them feel appreciated.

Dead crickets scurry under feet and are swept
off Lake Michigan. Floating the shoes of thought each song
is given to be gotten
back again.

To be alone in the lights in the distance is to be in
the light of remembrance,
but not yet song.

Sing the crickets' legs which are found
on clothes and ghosts. after the light in
dark, the pupils lost
like balloons over Kansas..

You think this is a fairy tale.

                                    You have yet to be eaten.

Your plan: to be a sustained note.

Gathering wings and things and bells to ring you plan not to be forgotten.

you'll be found.
in weather,
rained

like crystal lakes and labor.

The sound is as it should be.

Abraham killed his lamb and said to another, go.

And there were more to come.

I came to a mountain with figments..
There the sun came over and read the land
and the desert was not of sand but dirt and grass.
The desert was dry, but not thirsty. There were plenty
of figments, and no reason to picnic.

At the wedding the figures
outside of it all.. the ring that was a forest,

The inheritance was put off. But, still,
there, in the air of the best
hill there were three or was it four?

The wedding couple kissed with legs twitching and breaking.
Legs were singing and breaking and the teeth of the couple below
were falling out and laughing a lot.

Faithful, the married couple gives change to the wind.

Gives cuttings and grace and absoluteness.

The forests are cut and so are their legs.

Somebody doesn't want them to sing, or stand.

Received upon the change, or change-less,
the choir is sedate.

The gods are forever or never and given
to notes of quarters or eighths and breaks and pauses.

Silence.
Is.
Not.
Gold

Or silver and simple like an occupation
or a calling.

War is begun. You see.
There's blood to be drunk.

These are some songs that some will sing.

Travel is a part of every hero's standing
and forests are examples of places to get lost.

Over the hill, there, see, there are rocks like crickets' backs,
and saddened. They heave only when there's heat.

They still in snow.

Clouds are something to sing about. There above, shifting over,
and around to sometimes show you the sun.

What's happening is
turning over and over and over again.

The feeling of a record.

The need to exchange this for that.   fall the leaves are left
like cricket's wings shift the weight
of this planet carefully. They sing to cicadas
and the cicadas scream back with electricity
lighting the whole plane up.

Up 30,000 feet you'll see where they sing
each to each and play for keeps.

Take note. Watch your Feet. Dance.
Mirror and dance to each section/ di
vision. Vivisection.

Play your legs make music. Move. Encore.

                              All the trees are falling down falling down falling
                    down
[Over the hills the trees are rolling down and now it's over.

I'm done said the meat to oven.
I'm done said Lancelot to Elaine.
I'm done said the grass over-watered, still drinking.
I'm done.
I'm done.
Fare well. Good bye. Good bye.
I'm done.

I know, said Elaine. You're done. Here's your baby.

   The ghosts begin to gather and you remember
your heart murmur.
   Your heart murmurs.

Buzz. buzz. buzz.
Ssszzppphhhllllliit.
                    Ba-bump.

I'm done. It's time to gather rest under duress.
It's there forever. So get it done. I'm done.

Simply set yourself against it.
Rest against it. This tree.
Just for now and write this down.

I implore You, write this down:

       It is 12:22a.m and there's nobody else in the world.

March. Left.

       March. Right.

              There's nobody else in the world.
You're done said the meat. Get to the oven.

If you don't hold it like an egg it'll slip.
You'll hang it over the plate.

You want to see it stick
right in the glove. Not break.

One thing to remember:
You're on defense most of the time.

Careful now with placement and direction.

Hold lightly to what got you here.
From Durham to Tampa Bay.

In sun or dark or shadows made by others:
(F)actualize and fabricate and cut the shit from the day.

                         Put your fingers in the right place.

            Watch how it rises, turns or sinks. The tern.
in water.

Watch how the grass grows in four hours of play.

See how the fences came in.

All the crickets, then, have been chopped up in the lawnmower.

        CRESCENDO!

Hatch a plan.
Hold onto your friends.

It takes a good field crew to play the game.

You have to give to get.
                              It's never proven true.
The numbered footprint stickers
make your feet move like horse hooves
turned to glue. Horse-laugh. Toothy-face.

Look, can't you see, you never got a beef with me.
                              No mood for romance.

Look, can't you see you've only got to dance with me?

The floor is open. Take my hand, I'll take yours. This,
trust me, is nothing like High School.

You've only got to dance with me.

Eventually,
you see.

You've only got to dance with me. Eventually, we'll
all hear
the same song.

You'll see.

I hear the buzzing, yes.
I hear the bug zapper zapping. I remember
Haley's Comet passing. Yes.

You've only got to dance with me.
I'll make the music. I'll
make the song
you've already heard before
and bless me for being new.
For stealing you,
like no other.

Coral ambiguity sets singers overboard. Sometimes.

Sometimes that's exactly where they should go. If you go with them
                                        I'll understand.

I've seen the bones sticking out of the water;
I've seen silky fishes too—

the sirens of Odysseus
and all the beautiful women's mouths.

I wouldn't mind being tied up from time to time. To the mast.
Amassed in the listening.

            Get me to a boat—an ocean of limbs. I'd like to feel
the fingers crawl all over me and tug at my tongue.

The rowboat goes on and
on and waits for this. Misdirection.

Row row row your boat gently—

            God screams, you scream, I scream..

It's where we're going. I won't ask you where you been.

Hopefully it occurs to me that the dance floor has a place for more
. than two feet, or three or four—the usual
foxtrot.

Put the ghosts on the radio and
get Ben Fong-Torres to interview
a forest of them over the side of the boat.

The ocean waves.
Floating shimmering leaves.

for Parker Zane Allen

Too many times tonight I've lost my cherry.

      My cigarette keeps breaking.

The smoke flies out the window and dances with the trees.
And the wind.
And the thunderstorms that keep raining.

Before the sunlight breaks and breaks the morning.

Before the lighting strikes and lights the evening.

  The hours gathered are kept in a paper cup. Drink.

All almost always dry and always singing.

The future will be mountainless. You'll see.

I'm tired now, so, please, go to sleep.

I have grown lengths of love since we started this.
And love is my vessel. Rowing with bitter hands
and music sheets under my teeth, steering
thru a strong summer buzz and cold winter calm.

We move on and above. Move above like clouds.
Not fog. Remove the tongue and body.

Removal of all that stinks up the room.

There are plenty of rocks to end up face first on.

Plenty of myths to land you in Sinatra's bed. Or Australia.

Gasping for breath in the salty air. Gasp 'n' die.
Docked.   A mile high.   Country mile.
Coroner.   Basket-Head.   Casket-Maker.

Dead upon the dirt that brought forth the rest.
From grass like the rot that was there first.

Jam-face. Jelly legged. And all-together animated.

Don't rock the boat. Don't rock the boat.
          Swing low, sweet chariot. Swing low.

Hang high the bright star and row. Hang high the star.
                    I want to go home.

Elvis, what happened? Did the voices hurt your head?
Were you strung out strung to the bow?
Did the sirens break your teeth and eardrums?
Did you feel your ghost steering the ship?

Blood-torn sideburn. Ripped lip. Loose tooth.
Magnetic.

Candy and Absolute.

Spelling Bees in the trees and swinging ghosts. Back and forth.

It's not as easy as it seems. With chapped gums. Real blood.

Real problems. Real relationships. With-
out any ghosts.

Hard to see the forest or the trees or the Me's or the You's.

Alphabetical. Recorded. Sounded in the forms of ample machines.
Tall buildings. Swinging ghosts. Satellites in orbit. Swinging ghosts.

Actual memories. Swinging ghosts. Tall trees and asphalt rain. Children born.
Swinging ghosts.

What's on your answering machine?

Swinging ghosts singing your voice back at you. The voices of your friends.

Ghosts trying to sell you something. Get your grey eyes back. Back.

Star certificates. Naming stars. Names for forgotten stars.

Recalled.

Swinging ghosts. By neck or cord. Swinging ghosts swinging oars.

(Get back in the boat.)

Get on the swing. The Playset. Re-
arrange your face before you kick in the tapedeck,

Now,
        pull the antenna out
      from under
the skin of your elbow.
                            And, bend.

                                        This
shadow and echo of singing
from monk-like figures
in underbrush. (What do You call them?)

                    You came from singing.
You're surrounded.

The chalice is full of your blood.

You taste it every day and that makes you sing sick. Sweet.

Honey honey beautiful baby. Sweat. Break/beat.

Mead. Musical meat. /a
                    planted
                        s-
                          eed.

Thank you
for being my friend. Thank you
for taking my hand. Some
sense of lying is essential to the equation.   In a bed of leaves.

(The Bed Leaves)_____COVER,
        the clover is showing A Saint's face—SHY)

Under October light falling sidewise.
You know the way the softness of reds and oranges are.
Creams in wake of eyes, physical diminishment
in the playground of your used-to-be. Young and lying.   Liars.

Thank you for taking this and not forgetting. Help in
burying the deep
trees is needed.
    The roots have touched your
feet and lick at your heels. \
You should be surrounded by limbs.

            Human skin stretching down to touch you bit by bit.   The sense
that there's something else up there,   and round the moon the
sun and Apollo are hearing you and coming at you with arrows.

That's the reason for this. The sun. Begin to understand. The sun.
The sun is where it all is. You're reaching toward it with the plants.
Your fingers are no different than the leaves of eucalyptus,
branches of ficus, the weeds, or the grasses.   Have you
noticed the way you've bent?
                              Head gone forward toward the light.
Hands gone down t-
                    oward the water.   Body moved side to side
with the tide.
            The light?
The light.   The light.

for Jeremiah Bowen

June-faced,
I am.
And without
occupation.

Do you under-
stand? Do
You
see what
I mean?

To know
where You are
is a mountainous
shadow;

finding
ways
around
with
blind Feet.

It's not
up to you
or Me,
it's up
to This.

There before
it begins
and there
when
it ends.

*

Then when
it ends,
like a season—
the fall or spring.

Something
other

than
summer.

Something
unto
another
actual
continuing

the shadows
are
extra-
ordinary

and fashion-
ably
late.
In year.

Their over-
abundance
in summed-up
significance

is un-
regulated
in this kind
of relation.

*

Theirs is nothing
Upon their face

Their Face is
Ample

Wailing up
And down

Faces ample
In facing themselves

Facing the backs
Of heads

The Crowd
Gathered inside

Your house
Like Tourists

From the Desert
To the Aquarium

Remember. Shadows.
Fall. With hours.

for Michael Slosek

Stand up, Eloquent Insect. Be spared. Stand up.
Angels in the bell towers will soon be down.
Eloquent Insect in tall grasses, raise a flag.
Shadows cover the ground and shimmy.
Stand by the water, the water wavers reflections in light
on closer things, moving human meat and song.

*

The sadness the shallows bring to several shins.
Upward the suffocated are breathing in ordinary air.
Eloquent Insect, move through feet and dirt. Stand up.
Cash in your chips while you're ahead and move your legs.
Mash teeth between unparalleled jaws and slipping
tongue, lost in lost bell rings and mottled thoughts of water.

*

Severity of sense and grass stains from early born lawns.
Tastes from the frog or gravestone Lazarus touched.
Eloquent Insect, raise the dead and the lost bracket of
humanness, fascination, the face first up from the waters.
Gratify, Eloquent Insect, only what needs gratification
and hold it forth against evenings and dust, born through
an avalanche of beginnings lacking certainty of capping.

for Jason Attig

Forever gratified by the gathering
around a Table. Given to sense
of Sea and Land, a touch of belonging.
Men and women, together. The
whole of flesh bringing holy matter
to light, lit by walls or flame. Apollo
fashioned with rays, fashioned with
blinders to his own brightness watches.
Watches made by Apollo collect time
in bits of heat and light. Around the
Table, down from the attic, up from the
basement, sing pieces of human skin
lit by Time. Together in a moment,
insect and Man make a movement;
find both paper, sound, and song. Up
from the grave the dead can dance.
Inside the grave flesh still makes sound.
Crack and crinkle. Paper on shelves.
Fouled out, the song no longer sung.
There isn't time to bunt on such a count.
In the box, therefore, still able to
play. Tenses and pronunciation. Swing.
Syllable heroes in armor lacking a few
elements. The Fear. Where in dark lies
Women and Men. The Fear. Outside
ghostriders and few dry; sweating
insane, poured down the drain,
the rain, the rain.

In rain, wind and trees, elephant thoughts,
bits of bees and leaves; winged loss; wind in
tree branches, winds that leave behind
their loss in rains and things; the winds gone
over ever falling lashes; lashed the rain against
windows with branches; the lances pulled
over, when the wind ended,
a new movement:

S c a t t e r e d

This poem. Rain and
wind all over and sounding,
often, unnatural in their surroundings,

surrounding man and woman.

Its repetition and gratuitous excess.

Wet sex. Act in it. Accidents.

Surrounding. Magnetic to sound.
Sound and force and Source.   The Well
Gasping for breath in the shallow end.
    The waters continue to grow. Despite.

A respite from this shall be had. At End.

Mastered. Full. Sensation. All. Tables. Covered.

Ran over. Feet. Run over. and. ove.r.

Cars in the driveway for a Wake. Awake. A wake awake. Awake. A wake in the driveway. Drive way by the Lake, a Lady awake in the lake away. The Wake in the Way. A Wake. Awake in the Wake the dead are all sleeping. Gathered for the living walking, breathing insect wings. Drinking in the Wake, the Lake water. Awake. The Wake is for driving away. A way from the driveway the Wakeful waking are in the Wake away from the lake, the lady, and the wake. Their Dead are dead for some Reason. Reason in the Drive and Way for a Wake, awake. Wake beside the Dead, await all ways. There is no other Wake, or way, only hours of it.

for Michael Koshkin

This is not Classical, and turning into a tree
won't get you away from all This. I'm sorry.
You're lost, or stuck, or found in the same place.

It's here where you rest and here where you stand
and work and play. You have no way to get away
from the fondling, tickling, and preying or praying
of this game. You weren't ever a Virgin, anyway.
Get over it. Get in the game. And get on with it.
Play play play.

Dammit, Play. Play the song and sing along and get
in line and move your feet.

Dance.

Dance dance dance dance.
Dance to the Radio.

You have feet and personal embarrassment to use.

Dance.

Grapefruit move more in wintertime than this.

Move.

Get through the section where the music depresses,
and slide through the grasses with microblade graces.

Groove.

Hit the hi-top and split the rhythm.

Bang the hard head
and move the backboard.

Move the backing. Change the setting. Get in the mood.

THIS ENTIRE POEM IS ABOUT SEX.

Now,
believe that.

for Matthew Arnone

"The more you ignore me"

Oh, you're wasting your time. You'll
eventually listen.

"You're wasting your time."

I'll be in the bar, essentially a part
of your mind's linescape whether
you care or not. I've got your mind
in mine. My mine isn't mine or what-
ever in the area of gathered Tables—
in fact, it's all over and how can one
call the scattered debris of this and that,
the newspaper collage and old wall paint
in layers a singular thing or ever think it
to be. Go on and get. Get into the Box.
Swing away and miss. You never learned
how to hit the curve and you never will.
That's for Big Leaguers only. And only
will you then see how the pitch is coming
at you from where you sit; in the stands;
with clapping hands; clap-clap, clap-clap.

(sign) APPLAUSE

Garden children. One kills the other learning to harvest.
Singing a dead language, still singing. Dead children.
Unborn masses, or fatal Abel able to disable the fable.
Unable in broken swan song, fiddle and riddle. Girls.
Untended land, tended to, untended, tended to and dirt is under dirt.

Grass the hands of strangers. Sand the faces dropped from ether.

Lovely little batches of bundled words. Crickets love them.
Crickets take them, play them backwards, eat them,
throw them up into song and we listen.

        All the time. If you listen.
There's no non-sound,
  even when you're dead.
       You'll listen.
     You'll hear.

Moved teeth. Moving
teeth. Teeth
slipping
past the gums
and out
   over
   land.
Now's
the time in the
Christmas Carnival
where it's fun
to crucify
the bits
of things you love
against any movie script
and divorce.

   Yourself divorced.
   Easily in Las Vegas
     against the
     False Statue of Liberty,
     and the Real Elvis
       mocking it.

Jesus played guitar and so did Mohammed.

Baptized beneath the sickle moon each suck the moon for life.

Lifted down the Liffey they remove their easy limbs,

before entering
the ocean.

Gone into riptides and gills of fish and mermen.

Abyss and depths of watery semen.

Ghosts of gradual forgetfulness called creeks and lakes;

stagnant. Moving, finally, to the Mississippi or St. Lawrence

down,
or up. Up and down and figured in the making.

Taking in the occupation. Taken into consideration
for advancement. The winged breath taken back,
back in, back.

Moved like water. Weather. Moved.

Moved like the river before the land.

Sand-faced and thirsty. Gathered. Gather. Leaves.

Simple swing of the hand. Flick of the wrist.

In the game of song, in.

Play a tree for a little while
and wither from the love of a god.

I'll be there, climbing your limbs,
picking your fruit, making flutes
from your branches and finding
you ridiculous.

for Brandon Brown

Get it
Like the movement

of piano.
Minimal.

The movement
in ear

tripped this
way and that

formally
embarrassed

enough
to turn red.

Gathered notes
and leaves.

Ranked high
signals in night.

There the ping,
there the bass.

Over rooftops
equal grace

each evening,
or dawn.

Sampled rainfall,
sampled seasons

left in
pieces

taken whole
in the face,

ears, mouth,
nose and eyes.

Answers checked.
Spirits beautifully

out of key, in-
visible. Days

go by. Visceral
shapes; organs.

for Paul Hoover

"I don't want to remember you."

The sun will blow its fuse and when you wake up I'll be gone,
staring at a clock in the darkness through orange slated blinds
from an age unnamed and lost to history and mankind; simple
flesh will lack the will to look upon the distance I have reached.

It's due to the present, which makes it more embarrassing. Strangers
and cobwebs are left everywhere in shame. In bed. In the mouth
and between the teeth where they're hard to get out. To make.
The Californian hour is earlier, and sometimes more perfect. Time.

Out here. Outside of This. Where are you? Where is anything?

This is all, but time is kept by human skin like alcohol in a flask.

You'll get faced.

The hour will pass and you'll wake up in wrinkled clothes and skin.

Rumpelstiltskin bowls over and cashes the thunder in for another day.

He should have moved to Boulder. He'd never need to sleep but wait.
                              The skies
move over rocky mountains, collide and sound like what makes
you believe in something other than your own vocal box. Something
so fragile and easily lost. But to be against hills and hear Echo sing.
It makes you hate Narcissus no matter how much you may resemble him
in public pools or reservoirs or distant lakes. She only wanted to make him
hear her and the meaning of one means something in response to friction
and reverse magnetisms.

How nice it is to stand naked near a stream outside the forest and
hear a voice echoing, echoing. How simple it is to hear the insect
song and know they sing each to each and outside to others unintentionally.

Graves are often beside highways and freeways. It should make sense.

In fumes you'll see your face. Wavering. Pristine against
the white lines, and asphalt. Serene in the rubber hum and
in escape from insect buzz not yet lost.

for Steve Orth

"It sounded good off the bat."

Slow roller to third. The ghosts in the grass got in the way. Eyre
got the ball down. Just what the Giants needed. What the water
grants in summer, in June. In summer and early fall the way the
water moves from giant ghosts to simple song from man made mouths

Dominating the West. The west controlled by Giants' hands
making waves. The game a little bit closer. Snow in the air, at the plate,
and melting on the lake. Time to meet the Lady. With the lead
cut in half. To take the sword shone. Shining in the moonlight
and snow on the water. A walk. Lead off on second and first. At
home, the Hero thinks he knows what's coming. In a blink.
A swing. Bad pitch. A ball. Game over. The snow melts
in the air and the clear sky.

To spice her, anon, known not to bat an eye.

*

To die in an elevator with the lead in the ninth. The sound
of the crowd deflating and leaving on escalators and stairs. Down
and out of the stadium, no song. No singing. No song reckoned.

But song from the other side obnoxious in Pride. Song often in
Pride.. Songs following the out. Songs after the swing. Songs soft
in the correct decision in the Field.

Felt-Table-Rules. Touch only as much as you should. Drive toward
right field, and watch It go out. Gather your runs and breath,
and a decent percentage for your making.

Don't come home without your uniform dirty.

for Kevin Killian

In the house clean hands are forsaken. You haven't earned your keep.

Outside, in the grass, the locusts are making sense of displaced sand.
Chirps in the day turn into cries
under a darkly lit skyline.

From rooftops' green lights and gravity. The best broadcast available.

Better than the fourth inning, full of pop ups and ground outs.

Unfolding masses like unfolding lawn chairs uncrossing their legs
and taking the rest for granted,
the other masses amassed for another song of leaving. A prayer to the wind.

"Breathe in, or suck in, and take it. No matter. It's over. Game over."

November.

It's crazy and hard to listen to. The rooftop closeness,
and its distances. Backlit faces.. Manicuring a forest
between their ears. Unlearned. React. A deficit.

You should know by now
that anything can happen
in the 9th.

A diamond mine. Shimmer fluorescent blue waters.

In between Pacific and Atlantic. Great railroads,
moving caskets
                        into the ground,
back up again,   and across
for ritual comparisons.

This game doesn't end until there's a winner. Get back
                            on your rooftop
                                and
                            listen.

Plant a forest in the backyard and eat dirt. Get used to it.

Unborn,
            in a sense,
you've always felt
            the presence
        of your ghost.

                        Not at

    your back
but in it. At
  the spine
      a little twinge
and tingle. A
            small chill
or flush   for no   exact   reason.

Each treason.
Bred in.

Kept incubated in a box
with yellow eyes and skin.

                    you thought yourself

        alien
        before
    you knew the word.

Where'd that come from?
                    A blurry
                vision
and diseased liver
concentrate for thought.

                    A mixed tongue.
                    Forked.
                Mind. Little divots
            of afterthought
        from where where.

Snow walks.

The diamond inside the Forest.

Happy Birthday.

You're not even there yet.

SEND YOUR BIRTH CERTIFICATE TO THE CRICKETS IN THE TREES
AND SEE WHAT THEY THINK WAIT FOR WHAT THEY SAY

You have to do this early rather than later. They need
to know whether to write a requiem for Mozart or Salieri.

It doesn't matter. Don't murder your masters

or stop listening.

Put an ear in a cup and leave it.

No. You'll end up in a field where the sun sets and rises.
Where swings set motion in the air unpeopled. Distance,
or closure, whatever the borders be, be the same. The bees
buzz in. Bees buzz out. The teeter totters and the grass sways
in the weight of crickets and ghosts and angel wings. The sunspots
the sun gave are angel kisses and magical. Find the corresponding
shapes and match them. Watch the light break. Over field or ocean,
or a National Park. The trees, they're all different.
Why not hold hands and pass the time.   *Sppssst.* Pass it on.
By the end we've played a game of Telephone and it's all a mystery again.

Translation from here is always there to be there as it came here. It's
trans-lation. The movement of language over breathing tongues that
kiss in daylight.

Order for simple sequences of movement.

It goes from Here to There. And is there. It's there, always.

Sometimes poorly. Sometimes one moves from one place to another to find
the tree, and eats. Sometimes the tree eats them. Sometimes it's Adam and
Adam eats Eve, but not before Eve eats him and cages the serpent.

So's it's movement. Improvement.

Palindrome. Separated in the other in. In the other other other of.
Repeating notes
of pleasure not meant to resemble. Saturation of index.
Pages and pages of this.

From no where there there.

Oh, to be in love again! To feel each second live!
But it's nothing. No. No, it's nothing. It's something
that something feeds on. But it's nothing. It's something.

To sit in the dark and wait for the ballpark to open.

To blank out the evening with a good set of teeth and fists and drink.

To balance out each check or bass line against the boat's anchor.

Anchor set and pulled. Pulled up and out. Pushed down and into
the sea's floor. Pull up now. The sea life can rest again. The anchor's
up. The surface, now, is full of waking. Waiting for the exclusion.
The pull-out. The splash after the splash from the drop.

Awake in the balance. Planets rise and drop. Apollo sits still. With
wreckage festering about his shins with screams of starlight gone dim.

Nova against supernova. Against birth. Afterbirth.

Wet new in screams gone. Bastard.

Held high and hit hard. Sing.

Scream. Ring. Saturn sifts the sands of billions'.

Bastard beat. Lone melody. Cling-cling. Cling. To air and water.

Gather in each and wait. It's all on repeat. But you won't have a second chance.

Sunlight to moonlight given its all by the other. Or not. A mismatch. Mistake.

Surrounded in a forest of aftermatter. Wet just in the waking.
In the beginning.

Let go before the plunging. But in it.

Tongue-kiss and separate. Labeled likely in any event. Rabies
or otherwise. Says the machine outside. Says the machine inside.

You'll see. About time. In gravity where death counts rise
in every clean and clear sky populated.

Overly. Brimmed out.

Shadows, "we'll cover. But only for so long."

Gripped to slick corners. Soft curves. Watched the shimmer drop.
The waves rock. The anchor drop and raise. The leaving and the gotten.

The wet mouth to the dry. Sweat in bed. In ice.

for Beth Lemon

Monks were somewhere in This. Scrolling through the Internet, probably.
Cashing in their chips at the chanting tables, ahead by a prayer. Folding now
their robes before hard beds. Song outlasts. Sentenced to absolutions. Solitude.
A great fear and light. Before the night where one's been down, bedded down,
criss-crossed the road and velvet sun. At the back of Hope. On top. In tune…

Battlement days breaking like San Francisco in summertime-
expected-quakes. Swords swinging like tongues and shaking the tops of things.

And I think you understand Song, by now.

You heard it as an unborn in the womb before your ears were made. If not,
you're hearing it now, just somewhere else less anchored. A forest.
One where leaves are made of honey, and bark is skin good
to fall asleep against.
                Or bleed.

Granted. I'll take this song for its point. That is the point. I'll stay here,
thank you, and talk to you from here. I can listen from here, see? That's
the point that I've been dragging. Convincing you through them that I
can be Here. Now. And There then. Later. Some other time, I can talk
to you with equal matter.

We can sit down, now, you and I. Any time.

After that, the silence of the world. Until teeth mash and begin
to disintegrate before the rest. Before the rest. Before arrest.

Echo brings back what you left and leaves it there until
you yourself have discovered it and talk back. Back.

You'll get enough of it, but never enough. Dating into the song.

Dating the song is pointless. But this is not? No. Not? Who knows?

Your nose is perfect but hers isn't and somewhere someone
is having plastic surgery in a different change of notes left behind
from childhood.

Plastic basket. Bicycle-luck. Lucky braids and in-breathing.

Echo moves forward from the street and hums. Hums the street.

Echo moves forward from the branches to the streets and hums.

Hums the bees. Hums the street.

Echo moves forward by her feet from yours. Hums the stereos,
hums the keys.

Echo moves forward toward your face. Kisses your lips.
Kisses mine. Lips left here. Mine on hers on yours on mine.

On mine.

Echo steps back and takes the forest back in her arms as she
thinks, right Now, that she's lost both of us.

No. No. No no no. Echo. No. We're not lost. Come back.

The light's still on.

I didn't know you didn't know that song.

But how could you not?

There's shadow up.
Shades on sheet music.

Toys in the basement are throwing up. Bent over
like doubles of those that abandoned them. Vomiting
the same things, chunks of this and that similar to the
way their children would be. Gargbage-Pail-Kid-face.
Zitty Zane and Pockmarked Paul. Gathered together
in the November hall in the late afternoon where
the light fails and falls and causes a sense of weightlessness.
Crashing down, these astronauts are cushioned only
by the plush, neon carpet of the city skyline. Get on.
Go on, get on. Get out of here, away from forests, into
the bright lights and flash of city life.. For a while.
Row your boat out. Go. Get. Gather in the second
chance at life you get only once. Get it now while
the getting's good. Gotten. Get. It's not over yet. No
not yet but getting closer. Move over, Rover, the sound
of the world is coming over. Get over to the other
continent and let tongues touch. Take not the granted
but gather in the forsaken. Clouds gone grey and
dirty. Betray the white-bright halo around the
sensation of waking; but don't wake up swinging.
Keep both eyes open even during prolonged periods
of immobilization. When hearts begin to burst all over,
surround sound, hold tight and watch. Burst after burst of
star-red springs, spring forth. Set forth only after the creation
has granted access. Sample, first, each taste from each
spring. Decided that stagnant can kill and below
toys are clicking their lungs out; listen. Rooftops.
Lick your gums.

for Larry Kearney

Oceanic,
this world, round and blue, is not redundant, is, yet, to make mention of it.
Girls ring round the roses, and we all fall down. Goddess of this world. Certain.
The ocean starts backwards, from the river. Circe. The river is an anti-
beginning. A founding/ a foundry. A way of living to keep
the essential moving, moving. Certain. Round the waters the breakings taking
notice, the pushing against the banks..

In the Colorado sky the bowling game continues and the rivers,

> somewhere,   here,
>   there,
> or elsewhere,

shimmy in their shine.   Shake

in their dance
> and continue

an embrace of water
and land that makes
animalkind gracious,

> but not of grace.

                   When the sky pours down.

The overflow, the
way the banks are broken.   Absence of separation.

The pins are split. Hit. Big Hit.

No strike. No spares.

BIG FUCKING HIT!

We love it. We've loved it since 1959.

It doesn't matter how far you go. You're never far enough.

The song in the diamond is not the song in the rough, nor even close to the sound. It's almost nothing, now. It's almost as if we hadn't begun.

Fern.
Apple.

Whatever.

Fondly the way the sun sets, and leaves change. Fondly.

Row. Row, row, row.

Go and find yourselves upon the limbs.
         Levers to be pulled.
Albums to be made.
Record. Record.
 How awful. How full. How tear-able the pull. Hold. Hold.
Pause. Record.
Sip from the water of moving rivers. Move.
Set.
Sift.
Roam.
   End up broken on the telephone, or bank-side. Plenty of reason, left to behold. Old telegraphs and DOS programs in the limbs of some Commodore forest.

Shit, when do we speak,
directly?

It's hard to tell.

Grab a drink.

We'll make a pitch. A sail.

Sent the window to the door. A lot stolen, then. Away,
and looked in. Sentinel sound. Alarm and warning. Round
round, a-round. It's like the roses and the ring fell down, the
children all with posies in their pockets and the idea that Jazz
isn't dead. All fell down. Down. Down. The downy cover
of an album cover. Down down down.

Electronic age, magnified. Oh so understood the way the rails
of the MUNI moved. NOW. now. and NOW. the rails rolled,
under the wheels move. Groomed streets, impoverished, for.
Movement. The sound. Ground below Taraval would rumble,
rumble. Echo come back to San Francisco, she thinks, I want
to recapture my early adventures. For keeps. The trains keep
moving her catch. She catches. The game outside each
movement. Each scent. Sent telephone lines down. Down.
Down. The aerogram from the postal region of the Sunset. The
sun set, down, down. Mail all over from the mail truck. The
sound. The sound. It's in the air, today. Air is away. A way.
Away. Then Echo has no choice. No voice. No voice.

No. Nor do I. It's like an invader at the window.

A Space Invader.

for Helen Lhim

Score
for the movie
that is
happening. The score is happening.

See it happening.
The Hero is on.
The anti-hero
is yelling from a car at strangers on the sidewalk.

Nothing flinches. No light poles or gas stations. Nothing moves at all.

Nothing attendant at the moment of incapacitation.

Salutation, the ghosts of the present are now asking to leave.

> Let Me hold on to them. Who
> is Me, is me.

Is the same person, put together. Balsam, feather, wax.
Suntanned and good at math.

> It's not the same now or ever. Give in to the string movement
> of the crickets in the forest that you've left and can't get back
> to. It's gone from you forever, from us. It's gone and there's
> no going back except for this, or sometimes, That. You see,
> you've heard it, and you've come, and gone. It's not always in
> the evening, or in Love. It's sometimes, almost always, a
> complete accident, and There. Forever is no joke, but it
> sometimes seems to be. You're in it and you're not drowning
> but swallowing over and over and over. Choking. Alive. The
> movements of your muscles, unimaginable. Sensations in
> parts of yourself before unnoticed. Characters in your head
> now recognized gone lost and forgotten. Forbidden territory
> in a semi-abandoned land. The sounds of sex from the radio,
> out the window, and Echo in your head. Ring, ring ring
> ring.

Phones are not answering. Or answered. Acapella voices breaking the wires.

Celebrity through the waves.

Push in. Go in now and push.

Dip your head, breathe in, look up and say, "Apollo, your techno is sometimes annoying, but your concertos are often enjoyable and I wish you the best of luck in finding the love of your life at the least of your touch. God knows we all do.

Dee-do." Now into, Pacific.

for Lauren Shufran

I want to spend time.
I want time to be spent.
I'm pent up in spent time.
I have spent time in San Francisco. Rent.

I am in about.
In the ring around the forests.
The forests all fall down. No Knights
are true
to the Table Round. No. None.

Lancelot kills his brothers and grieves little
for the death of his son
in Africa.

Rimbaud crying about guns. Guns. *Buy 'em if you gottem*.

Golem gone mad. Made mad.
Mud made.
Mad made.

Machine math.
Mechanical library.
Forest of levers and cranks.

The forest turns the terns from the beach. Turns.

Game done, unforgiven. Saddled satellites for orbital rides. Ridden.
Circled. Sound. Sound. Circled. Circled. Sound. Damned. Circle.
The Waves about your ears killed Elvis. For a minute.

Thank God for car stereos. Water fou-

tains,

tall beers, baseball, free love, blink-

ing lights.

Las Vegas University.

Suppose a chorus. Suppose the experience. Suppose the world
were wrapped around us (You and Me); yes, this is the point in the poem
for a little romantic interlude. This part, here, is for you and me, Beth, you
and me. Whoever You shall be. In the chorus waves the ringing ears. In
the Oceanside sense of here, belonging, and longing, the longing wins.

Come back, come back, come back before it's too late. My love, it's too late.

My love the ghosts are absent, or too abundant. My love the air now could
suffocate.

Bubbles in California are bursting over the coastal waters by the billions.

It'll be the end of a country. Sardonic value in a graveyard ant farm.

Tunnels' sound. Built. Building bit. This romantic part is left to rest. Is
here to be left, unfortunate. The sadness of it, right? Unpardoned.

No embarrassment. No red to the ocean or scent of pine from the forest sent.

No sign.
So song. Waiting for the song.

Here.
Hear it till the end now. Now.

From the start.

Go on. I've got your heart. Remember. This was the romantic part.

You've got mine.

That's why I'm dying.

"Start. Start. Don't let's start."

The album of a beautiful ending.
Lots of trees in the setting. Perfect for a summer wedding.

Hold my hand. Gravestone-heavy. Ghostly takes on a different dimension/
description/ handle on the radio.

Breaker. Breaker. Waves and leaves.

Grab bag. Big Apple. Alphabet. Tuition.

"You can call me Betty."

Giants of this and that go tumbling through the forest for the trees,
knocking down each and breaking limbs,
hospitalizing each other and visiting when they can with
flowers and candy and vodka for the Jell-O. Gone through the trees,
knocking down, planting seeds, and having
plenty of sex and love under the sun, sometimes
far away
from the ocean, far away from the roiling river, the fish's
fever, the accidental occident and westerly winds. Their
hands so large they mimic their ghosts,
the air and the wind, the sand and the dirt,
the movement in the canopies and birdsong
sung about their eyes or at their shins. The rings,
the sins, palpable palms, the movement of South,
the catering of Central, the certainty of the coast:
West go left, East, east, East go left too and gather your
governors in a hall to battle, or play chess. Descent.
Down. Down. The Giants' hands are now full of diamonds.
Accidents. They die sometimes and turn back into coal. Kiss
a Goddess each chance they get; they have such reach and
big eyes, there's no such thing as resistance. Their one-eyed
cousins, against Odysseus, though, found different, and threw
rocks into oceans for a Tidal Wave. Sound the ring. The alarm.

We're there again.

for John Sakkis

I, and if by I, I mean Me, I sometimes don't but sometimes do.
I and Me and you are now ready together. Gathered
and not yet forgotten, the I is in You and You in I and Me; there,
all ready; there, without absence; nor tardiness; Here, You see. Here.

It's a game and not a game and has everything and nothing to do with how you
play.

Press Me. Press Play. Press Again and again and again.

Send Love and Poems. Send History and bits of leaves
from trees you've seen.

We need a Name.

Give again and I'll take. Take now the way I take from Them. Here.

In this. In this like a river, which is an allusion to itself in this poem, thus,
now, no illusion. There's no illusion but the shapes in the corners
of spaces you cannot touch. For fingers broken by insult, and the lingering
of the bitter shade near windows and rooms.

Empty pianos and lounge singers. Sad sand. Sad sad sad.

No giant illusions, or impulse in this pulse. Pumping. Pulse.

Sadly on and on. No end in sight for this where water does not move
into water but bones and graves and grass. Duncan's grass had
a lot of this, but different. It's all bones and sad. Sad.

Old men and old women die before this.

Old things are still around and left for almanacs.

Set tables.

Families in America talking about nuclear capabilities in the ghost of twilight,

I need you. I need you in two of two. Two of hearts.

Cold loving the hot coal.

Bodies burning. Desire.

I need you.

for Chantelle Patterson

Beating organs dropped; left in water. Blood. Teeth.

Placed back in. Back out. Dropped. Down.

Down the organs go. The ants go marching. One by one.
By the river's edge, outside the forest where
the afterbirth is left. Where bone is often broken and water mysterious.

The keyboard rings. Sound the music again. Synthesizing. Siren.

Staccato. A beat. A good rhythm section, now, in the chest. Before
the spitting of blood and whiteness gone from eyes. The drum.

Bass line of basic breath. You've breathed. Down. My breath
in the ghost's face.. Chorus wavering. Manipulated.

Outside of ALL OF THIS. DON'T YOU GET IT?

My guts are a-twist. The music. The fucking Music.
                    THIS for IT. TIT for TAT.

Got your music, then. The beat. It's all about. and amplified.

Sensual record. Certified and lost forever. Replaced by fear
for thrill of the chase. Each for Each and the doors for wandering.

Opens. Shuts.
                    Shuts in the face.
Against horizons. Scene. Lines. Differences and facades.
Mountains against.

Tackled by the tabernacle. An army. A choir.
A Tubeway Army.

"Where have they been?"
"Whose birthday is it?"
Get the blow-ticklers.

It's England. 1977.

In the new wave, the covering. The way This has moved away, from the Forest, to Water. Which is belief?

A Hell of a Earth. Never learned.

Power chords with the fuzz turned up and notes lost, or gained.

Fade away. Not Fade Away.

Good bye. Bye bye. Goodbye.

Salutations. Goodbye.

Goodbye. Got to their goodbye. God, goodbye.

Hallelujah. Goodbye. Sound out, now. Sound loud. Set the constellations afire. Buh-bye. Good bye. Goodbye.

Set them up and knock 'em down Bye bye.

This is evolution. Bye bye.

Bye.

for Ben Fong-Torres

The movie isn't over.

It's the never-ending story gone on again with cricket song
and ant hills, and David Bowie in the background. Among others.

"Let me fly away from you. For my love is like the wind."

Leaves. Left. Go Left. The left in the world. What. West?

No. Left? Left. Left? Left. Right? Right. Now, Left.

Heart blown through the wind against the canopy tops the way
disco blew through the 70s and everybody'd like to forget. To forget.

Oh, Echo!

Leave me! Leave Me!

You Kiss my life. My Life begins. This is no End! Oh Echo come to me!

Come.

Come to me oh Come!

You Life, you know it, you know yourself like you know the wind in the leaves;
the way the air has come in and out of me; the way other's skin clings to each, as
creatures of the wind, wild in the wind, wild is the wind! OH ECHO!

Come.

for Katrina Walker

In an aspen forest, one root.
Over the mountainside, an aspen forest,
holding down the mountain.

In America, ghosts spring, come from the land
and spread and grasp each into each and build
some root, one root. The roots of the aspen
                              all grow into each.
Grow ghosts now in the middle of the country.
Call the nearest and ask if they can make their people into aspen. Wizard
of Oz trees having nothing to do with apples.
A little magic, please, now. Now and
then. There, now. Give the way for a little bit of touching. It's sexy.
Please get the underground. Get the way the things go outside
of the main stream, the mainstream, the way things usually go on the Top 40
station,
the way things have been reported; uprooted; neglect
the news and the papers and wait for laser surgery on eyes
to finally be perfected and get it to see. You see. Every breath
you take, every step you take, You are on camera.
Your fourteen minutes of fame, now, on Reality TV.
You're being watched.
You drowned victim.
With every step. the Police are Watching You. You,
though, are sometimes a Pop Song, and sometimes not. It's sad. Sad
how we all want to be rock stars, but are not. It's a calling.
A calling to say again and again, Please.

for Benjamin Hollander

72

Isolation. This joy division. This separation. From Land and Sea.

From tree to tree. The manic maniac is on the make. Maniac is making
the mark. The make. Sound in the trees. Your makers make, the maniac
makes in media, in air and space, in schools, and schools of birds and fish.

Fishing through the lake with silk threads of this you'll get only halfway.

Drunk.

Dunk the salamander you found and blame it on a poet
when the dead come back up.

Come back from it. The way the blame can come from anywhere.

Canopies to cover, in cover. To cover another's song.

Sound from out there. Something saying: I guess I've seen the sparks flowing,
like no one else has ever seen them flowing.

Not lost to the ghost in the grocery store buying apples from the trees
that threw down unripened ones upon the ones now picking. Basketing
the bunches in a T-shirt.

No punishment here. Not now. No, tourism, at the moment, is appealing.

Gathering leaves. Sadness in trees. Water cold everywhere. No Bahamas.

No reason for their weather.
                    Rain. inRain.

Weather. And don't speak of Spain.
They tell me. The weather there.
No. No reason.

Now.

A thousand feet in a second. Slow down. Slow down.
Other
wise
there's sometimes
no coming back to the ground. Ash in air. Bits
of junk in orbit. No
gathering.

Both Jesus and Zacchaeus hung from trees. But Jesus
hung from one in a group of three, a forest of wood and skin.

The tax collector began in the Tax Man by George Harrison and
was followed up by stories in the Bible. Rivaling this is the
way the blood of Jesus flowed from the tree amongst three,
the way three became a number later; or more. A number to
strike out or count on or make a wish. Granted, the blood flowed.
Dropped from a gaping wound in his side onto the dirt below
where nothing grew. Ever. No. And nothing grew there before,
either. It's the crown that fascinates some. Distant in the past,
in the present, bleeding from the gums
and the head, and side and feet and wrists. It's painful to be a
believer, in anything. And figurative. It figures. Southward
suns set. More suns on the way. Guaranteed by TV and
commercials and skyscrapers. Trash-canned.
     Get on the cross. Now. Gather your friends for stigmata.

Praise! Praise that nothing's happening. But the buzz
in the trees. Trees that continue to buzz and call and push us out.
Your hands are bleeding.
That's from the sun.
It's different when all of this is upside down.

A pound of flesh. A glass token. Expense.

for Jen Rogers

Busloads of lepers are coming to town for limbs! Land is
made for forgiving, and giving, and giving in. Get in. Get in the
bus and watch your teeth. Watch your fingers sway. Every night.
While the wolves are away. YEAH! Gather things to collect. Keep
everything. Get on the bus and wait for your nose to fall off. Pick it up.
Place it in someone else's handbag and place the funny nose and glasses
from the funny store on your face and SCREAM! Laugh then, and sing.

Wait for what the others do, but not too long. SCREAM again and laugh
and sing and sing. Then take the glasses off and place your swaying fingers
in the holes in your face and laugh. Until the wolves are away and the bus
reaches its destination. Appropriate city here or there
in California or Delaware, getting good the Good to be gotten. In there.

Passing faces off like death masks, gas-masked. Terrorized.
Passing faces. Faced and facing.

Sounds of skin crawling. Bugs over dry flesh falling. Leaves.

Panic attack at the back of the bus. Get in.

Hold hands and kiss and watch your lips fall off. Get in.

Give in and get in and give yourself up. Put your hands up.
Watch 'em fall off.
Love someone so much to collect their teeth
in a paper cup. Pick 'em up
with your last two toes left. Passive.
I've passed. Past branches, more roots gone rotten.
Under this.

Glass eyes rolled toward the bus conductor. End over end.
Over and Over. "All aboard the gravy train!"

Echo. My tongue drops to the floor.

for Jared Hayes

Oh, Lonely Gail and the Insect Song. Oh.

Wind through the whimsy, the wind went. Song sent. Sung.

Oh, lonely gale, only wind swept through the streets and trees tonight.

To touch each limb, and left.

Push each insect aside and sing. Or sing with.

Sing. The song that you were born to sing. The reason They
cut the cord. Chorded. Accord. In motion. E-motion.

Strings. Strung.

The lonely are only longing like Elvis in future days spent.

Waiting for the rain, killing time again. Waiting. Spent.

Sometimes: A little bit of background music.

Fractured, hands, touch so plain and stale to the gale that kills.
Disintegrate and find the cure. Find the pain, the ache that
makes us all wait. Wait for the rain. The ghost again. The crickets
and summer to come back again. A second sound to take over?

Hardly lost upon this fever. Guaranteed us forever. Touch the plain.

Strangle. Dances for the rain to come again and fill this human skin
with human blood made from things left below the grass.

THIS IS HISTORY.

In making, it's always in. In making. Hands down. Hands on.

Prayers and song. Sand turned over and on. Turned on. This poem, about sex
and love, and ghosts and gods.

Get over it. No stop stop don't let's stop.

No. Wait. Get over it.

No. Don't.

Can't in the beginning, end or middle.

Magnificent.

Listen…

There…

the song…

it's begun all over again and nobody else is in the room to have pressed Play or Repeat or Loop.

And it's from 1978.

Terrific.

for Armand F. Capanna II

Not the same as 1977, when there were brand new waves making this flesh crawl, and grow. Limbs reach outside each forest and draw water through Absolute existence. Existing like an alien in the police station or Airport. Taxi the runway. Double-parked.. Take a cab and don't ask the price to Ireland. Wait it out and count down. Lift off. From the past to the future, from the skin to the ghost. Get down. Launch. Get off. Get around and land safely. It's all about travel and how heroes were often in the mix of different landscapes. Mountains and castles. Prairies and fairies, damsels and towers. Handsome loot and hair to pull. Lots of sex for the making, if the making is to be caught. Shielded, armored, protected against the rain. The swoop and flange of the forest felt ways through, thought. Thoughtfully given to advantage by masking face in metal and beating down your brethren when appropriate. Then forgotten. All reason. Beaten. Beat. That's beat. The beat. In desert the cactus bloom. Shin guards and heavy toed boots for protection against rattle snakes in places like Brawley, CA, or elsewhere, where air conditioning keeps the living living. Old and feeble, the warbler and the warbled, the manic and depressed set against the sun, yet again, the sun and cicada loving it up living in the trees' buzzing.

Dear Mr. President, Again,
         electric afternoon, here
in Colorado, somewhere in a country on somebody else's map.

But who cares?   The spiffy swift are swiftly lifting up the invisible
to be reckoned
         and beckoned, recorded and taken in for granted,
         granting <u>love</u> and freedom, making it behind
the curtain

         and singing, MOSTLY,
                  in curse words,
the sheets wet with distance and forgetfulness. forgiven
and taken in as taken gets. Taken. Sands again, and pigs, and sounds again a bass
line
through this forest.

Leaves and limbs and lumber left rotten as the fruit that bore us. So bored.
The boars are
         rushing the forest floor,
         tearing up the leaves and graves of bones,
lost from decades, memory, or
anything that could care. It's not the same, anymore.
It's not like it was, anymore.
                  "Hey, pig. Piggy-pig pig-pig."
         Hey pig shut your mouth.
I'll eat your tusks.
                  If ever stuck on an Island.
                           Eat them first.

Get a good grip on their ribs before you rip.

for Alli Warren

Southern Belles in London sing and a gang of four drop drums and bass
and kiss each face that faces each. Now, an interlude:

> Today no Giant won in battle. A loss to every drifter. Every one-eye
> poked out by wooden spike, wooden bat. The rest rode out under sheep.

At home, or in the trees with their tax man.
Zacchaeus called in sick, though, and nothing counts today.
We count on him calling in every day.

The diamond field must soon give way. The field crew is ready.
They sway with eyes gone dull.

Rain delay.

Electrical storms and thunder. Mountains sprout. Plenty to sparkle.
Starlight, star bright.
From flesh, fields, broken ground. Lines lifted. Dropped. Seeded thought.

Sand in the face forgot the taste kicked up in each race in Greece,
Achilles and Patroclus eat each. And others gone mad under
a chariot wheel. Carousel. Fires. Ferris Wheel. Kiss kiss.

We know what happens.

Eat sand. Eat sand each eat sand that witch.

From the sand the Golem. Blood given enough. The magic
monster risen. Rises, above, us, all. In skyscraper majesty, and
capital. Magical in its beginning, and lasting. Sand from which it
came, came coastal, we all suppose. Constant thunder in the middle,
created much for its survival and remembrance. Settled in the bones.
Graveyard wary, the weary keep an ear to the stone and continue
to vote, hopelessly. Placed the ballot face. Faced and facing. Un-
attention. Intentional inattention. Accident. Unforgiven. Nothing
in the first books of this. Nothing. Nothing to tell US how to get
out of this. Stuck. Stung. Pig. Rung up the ladder without a rung to
get down from. How about this in a land of millions? And a ghost
born every day to tell each how not to live or how. And no one
is listening.

[It's the same old song since I was young and riding in the passenger
seat of my father's car, an old yellow, beat up Mazda, hearing Pop
on the radio and forever cementing the sentimental majesty of
soundscape and imagery, psychedelic furs and seagulls.

Each Knight is in the making making-out the night for lovers
and young hearts. Breathing in isolation in motoring vehicles.

New Jersey, or Boston.

"I'm doing the best that I can. Mother, try to believe me…"

Beauty in things I'll never describe, ghostride, ghost writer, this poem
in the hands of an other.   IT'S NOT MY FAULT
Real in this letter later formed.
And   no   one   is getting paid a cent.

for Jason Hackman

To be the pulse in the left wrist of the crucified Christ!

Sense of what's coming. What's leaving. What's on the ground.

In no responsibility for words spoken before the last beat. Breath. Rush.

Sensibilities in earthly, holy. 40 days and 40 nights of favorites played out.

No one wanted to be Jesus.

Sent gravestone fingers, a skinny neck to take
down the breath and bellows.

Hard hands of all prophets are made implacable by sadness and woe.

Favorable, it is. Favorable for sentence. A sentence. In sentence.

Sentenced, again. Placed in each tomb. Sentence

Left from the wrist, each drop, sentenced. A drop
in the cage, outside, or over the overwhelming well now. Welled up.

Well done in the air outside of amassed history. Labyrinthine.

Made for following, and losing. Oneself. Gained. Lost. Whatever.

But to bleed from the wood and the iron. Unreligiously, but holy.

Iron and blood.

To bleed from the trunk of a tree, unknowing.

Iron in blood. Mineral. Metal. Animal. Insect song.

Something of a prayer in the back teeth of a nonbeliever in anything.

Iron. Blood. Bark on the tree.

Wind out the window. Now. A thin violin.
Things we've played.
Out the air. Wheels' sound. Sent in sentence.

Time in doors. Shades in each room
watching and trying
on clothes before each mirror.

Carrying over the breath of another. Skin.
Lungs gone out an hour
ago. Gone. Timed out. Brought back in.

This is where the story ends. This is, no, not a story. There
is not a story in this. A dog barks at something
not there, is promised sparks, and glitter and
credit for seeing what we all don't see.

It is well-documented.

And is not "me".

There is nothing in this world that has not now been
well-documented.

But for that, over there.

Holes in This.

Cold spots.

for Becky Ohlson

The Green Knight can have my neck, without Gawain's green
girdle. I'll let my stomach out too, and laugh. I'll bellow out loud, so
loud, in fact, they'll hear me all the way back to 400 AD. Excuse me.

I'll pass over each prairie and dale, down to the stream and fill it
with the blood of my friends and enemies. Nothing new,
here, you see. Old stories ever and never collapsing.
Like Giants in the broadcast across the land making
earthquakes, and tooth aches, and false dementia to hospital the elderly.

I'll give the Green Knight my neck some night I come across an
odd hill down by the creek in a glen. I'll give my neck and let
my blood spurt out across the land to sing the song of a cricket
now found. Once found, then loss. Great loss. A giant land of crickets
turning things over, turned over on their backs and burnt by
countries and borders, and magnificent forests found to be too much.

I'll turn my head to not watch the ax. I'll be relaxed and breathe, and think,
"This is not horror nor anything to do with honor but a way to go
and begin to speak." And then will end my think. Blood gone brown
on someone else's hands and in the ground, over the mound by the glen,
in the dale, near the smooth running creek. So many trees. Leaves
to walk on. Not often stalking. Swinging. Winging. Ringing in a laugh.

I'll laugh and bat an eye. A bat. Hit .400 for the first time in years, and
bring down great things; evil things; and figure myself in the lot.

Power-balanced in the dark of the woods. A mentioned nightmare.

Cicada. Suggestion.

for David Porter & Antigone Michaelides

"Believe in me as I believe in you." It's simple.

Smash a pumpkin on my front lawn and call in a haunting. It's All Saints Eve. It's Halloween. It's candy teeth and monkeying, and wolves all let out.

Windows burn in jack-o-lantern lighting. Children embrace the fall of Heaven.

The star Lucifer diffused, let loose, let fall from the edge over, to here.

What some call purgatory, but not all. There's baseball, after all. And ghosts to keep things interesting. Biting off your ear when you don't listen.

SO LISTEN!

Jesus, this isn't so hard. Card tricks, magic fix, the fix in the brain. A grain of sand for a horse! My horse for a kingdom! I don't have either, and neither does this. Nor no one we know. In here, there's the sound now of cars gone by. Baseball on the radio, and the name of Jeff Carter ringing against the walls from John Miller.

You should be in San Francisco. A city bright, instead of this forest dark.

The black bugs all abound and on the walls. Nodes of this and none of that.

Corners pushing in all around. Nothing like the open pushing skyline.

Homeless reckoning they know the ghosts
far better than others. Ghosting about the gutters and doorways and Camelots of underpasses, passing by on crutches and stumps, and wings of breath and air.

Sounds familiar. Saved. To get a save in the ninth inning, you have to be in a close game, all ready.

We're all in position, all ready, to get a save.

Okay, all set.

Apollo at home with the big bat, and Her on first with the lead-off. Luckily today we have *The Breakfast of Champions* on the mound.

We all need a good closer now and then.

Who wants to buy a car?

Gash my neck, I say, he says, we say, you say, who cares? Cut my neck
and watch the broadcast of blood over this field. Shades outside the forest
have been waiting for this fall. Fell. The bell. Bell-bell. Ring-ring the bell. Angels
in the high tower are singing again. Christmas trees are ringing, giving wings
to angels in movies played on television. Actors are happy. Smiling and glee-ing.
Ringing. Shades in the living room are laughing against the floor. Sinking. Waiting
for someone to buy them a drink, or to do one for the other. Waiting. Sentences
breaking apart in the making, in the deliverance from still-birth and fleshly destiny.
Absence of cartography. Hallowed in the Name. Gathered together for songs of
crickets in jars, baking in summer. No winter, no fall. Now summer comes,
the light. Apollo, or Gawain, lifting their weapons with the dawn, growing weak
with the light. One makes lovers, the other feigns love. Situated all over the world.
Turning now, and burnt. Burnt at the states, the stakes, the meat over the grill. It's
2005, June 28, and their smokes still fill the sky. When clouds are close, or summer
hits south CA, and presidents say "it's worth it," it's there. Facing forward, never
back,
giving up what the light can't take. Color from the grass, grass gone brown. Fish
all asleep in their creeks by the mound. Re-placed.

Rephrase.

This has something to do with today. And grapes.

for Chris Grant

Lonely Gail collects along her way, pieces for the song.

Piano braces. Metal faces. Braces on the tongue. Song
for the radio, unable to not begin. Song about love,
about god, heartache, and other pop stars—inevitable.

Gail winds through the streets turning crickets on their backs,
and beetles too, tickling their bellies, making her way
for the hills and trees. Only to come back in a harsh wind
over Ocean Beach blowing out all the bonfires and the
homeless' hope of a cigarette or beer from the young
gathered around heat, in darkness and cold, for nothing.

Gail kisses the fishes and mispronounces this company.
The three in the corner with eyes like a pyre and so thin.
Going in and out like bad reception. Waving. The ocean.
The slight film of vision, and the sound too. Antennas
popping out of my brain calling these things over
whether I want them or not. Gail often now with guests.

Get out, get out! I say.

They wave.

We'll leave those behind, for now,
 with the dice, the eyes, and the ice.

However, that contradicts our move to Antarctica.

God bless. God bless. Adieu.

for Sabrina Calle

An imbalance stretching toward implosion. Non-release.

Thus: NO SOUND LEAVES TILL IT'S OVER.

Canceled each other out on the way out in the other. Sampled.

Mixed.

Re-mixed.

Programmed and channeled. Forever at the board.

Mixing board. Board game. Sands hands. Sans. Face. Mouth.

Shade coming in. From the South. Said, I'll be right in. Cover your mouth. No, no, don't cover your mouth. I'll be right in.

Slugs in your mouth, throat, stomach. Game in. Matter for the matter. Said soil in the guliver. Soil in the teeth. Meat meet meat.

Worms and crickets legs left as eyelash garnish. Shadows lengthening for youthful glances. Glancing the shade. Glint.

Gallant. Gigantic. Galahad with Jesus' blood in his hands. And none for us. None for us.

Sad sounds out of the mountains. Couples married in avalanche.

Millions, then. Then Billions.

Bulbous. Bulging a bugle call.

REVELLIE!

Then the world.

Covered in it.

Romantics were squashed by the 70s of what century, who knows.

Wedding gowns are thrown. Rings are blown. Up the mountain. Up.

There, wait… listen. No listen. The grasshopper is eating his cousin.

The shrub is wetting the fire. Land is raking the water.

(Air over the middle of the tongue. Splitting. Cold spots. Cooled.)

Cain is beating Abel with a ho. Something grows that looks like corn.

Something from the brown grass and dirt. Something else.

Eve is getting away with everything, and Lucifer is yet again a star.

There, look up. Against the sky, by the North Star. There, Up. Next
and faintly near it, another, called Lucifer. It's going by. It comes.

Goes. Leaves without a faint exit. A winding sigh.

Saddled in night, stapled to the sky. A cradle robe. Swaddled
like a newborn.

I'm in the other side, against the mirror's edge. My blood should now
be leaking out the cracks.

This picture frame of a forest. Pretty trees painted like the TV.

A holy grail thrown from the outside at me. The window I'm
pushed against, while I listen to some song. Cracks.

Pop. Cracks. There along in a crooked line. My blood. As plain
as it would be against the snow. Pooling at each of your feet, Apollo,
Arthur, insect, shadow, shade and dale. Grass and limb and river
of sails. Sailed out, sallied away. My rowboat lost in the tops of aspen,
somewhere in Colorado, or in glaciers. We meant, didn't we, to move
to Antarctica. But never did. We said it like we meant it but never went.

Penguins are no songbird to immerse in. Glaciers are brutal and
seethrough. Clear. Blue. Submerged.

Sand and mountain. Gabbles to break each tooth, too. You're so
afraid of falling teeth, fallen out, breaking. Loser in possession.

Game here in the shadow, where sun lights the diamond. The grand stand.

Gail in birds' beaks and cricket's hairy legs pushing.

Terrible accident. Aforementioned. Holy fail and the insect bell.

Sell! Sell! Sell!

This is an absolution from eternity. This is the inaction of eternal. This
is to make up for the loss from infinity minus this This. This
cradle rocked in Egypt by forgotten animals on hind legs. Gods. gods.

God gods. Gone from this now. No more ghosts. Gone. Gone and now
I'm forgotten in the lot. Neither home nor lost. Salutations
from the backbeat of gratitude. Sandaled feet in summer.

Crickets all over.

Covering. Choruses from the sheets. Chorals impractical and neat. A
drink to be had near windows. On porches, passed out in the street.

Mary meant nothing by it. And baseball didn't either.

When the cricket marries the grasshopper, the priest doesn't declare.

Baptisms are nightly and often in someone's hair, or touching.

Open windows to hear pop songs and listen to the movement of hair.

Blown. Outside. There. Gone and lost on me and stairs. Falling.

Missed and unmentioned, calling in to bother again. Hello, I'm here,
I'm in this again. I can't come back to work. No, no. No, never again.

I'm stuck in this other world and I'd rather be there, really, but I can't
work. No, nothing. Nothing from here.

Where is the step to the top of this tree? I can't make it to work today.

I'm off at the feet. Someone swept my leg like I was the Karate Kid.
I'm innocent and left out from the 80s and debonair. Not really,
but I'd like a second chance at this.

I'd like to try again, from here against the glass forest,
to make things, now, more clear. Now that I've seen
all I've seen from Here. Now there's this abscess, that
Absence. The absence in the beginning. From San
Francisco, Saint Francis, the animal kindness of Man.
Categories to manage, now handled and fair. I've

been there. I've maintained a certain appearance and
fought off each ghost with non-reluctance, only
feigning it, at most. At most. Well, mostly. At the well
of another. The other in here with me now is going
at it like no Other. I've had enough. I'd like to make
things malleable, amicable, and clear. Impetuous,
perceptible, sensible and without so much of this
fear that's rattled each back tooth and tongue from
you and me. I want to say that Love was here with
us but I'm not so sure it was. So I'd like to try again,
to let each know that no Jesus or Guenever were ever
really here, or I don't know. Sort of in the peripherals of a manic
depressive graveyard thought of special accident. The
masks worn to make a forest are only letters gotten
here through synapse. A beard. All so accidental. I don't know
what this was trying to say to the woods or birds or bugs
and things. I don't care. I think I thought that I had no
thought before this. This is the beginning. The plunging.
Head first. Now. Through the forgotten membrane and fear.
Veins. From here where things start. I've no recollection
of either this or that or there. Either, before. Afterbirth.
I'd like to try again. Before the end of this. Here
beginning. Again.

Give me another turn. I'll use all the limbs torn off through history.

Row the boat with the deads' fingers and feet. No, No! No,
I didn't mean curse. No, not at all. I'll row.

I'll row.

Sentenced to this now.

Watch. I'll row. I'll do whatever.

And give the evidence after.

Here. See?

I call out from the tops of the trees, say
whatever you ask me to say. Make me.

I'll bellow loudly and call "There Are No More Heroes!"
over and over again just like you asked me.

I'll do it again and again. Just let me rest.

For a bit. For a moment against some rock. Or mountain.

In a summer wind. A Breath without meaning. Nor meant.

Coming in, and leaving.

Just give me that.
A second's thought to my self. Mine own.

My future children. Whom I'll tell there are no heroes left.

None. Gone forever.

When what I really meant was that liver is stronger than the heart.

Gather your leaves in winter and burn them in the fall.

Scents are sent and remembered. Photographs for the angels.

There's something else. I meant,
My mother was not Mary and neither was yours.

My lover was not Helen.

The ghost is saying right now: Because You've never loved.

That goes against everything. You see? You see what
I'm up against. This isn't easy and I need a rest. A second
chance. And I don't want death to be what comes of it.

The fallow land and blood on brown grass gone brown with it.

Terrible accident.

I don't need a green axe to prove anything.

Or Giants batting .440 with 1200 trips Home.

Terrible here again. A second chance.

To come again.

To find another Try. A turn through the style

Fashionable, but late. And ready for the cameras.

But I forgot. This and everything before.

I promise.

Cross My Heart.

I'll wake up at the Start and this will not have happened.

Just give me a new number and pin it to my chest.

I'll forget.

Begin. Sound of breaking skin. Penciled in. Swimming.

I'll never be the mermaid's song or singing. For real.

Each reel in the John Peel Sessions erased. Forgotten. Lost.

Like all of this and what I've Got. Gone.

I promise.

Move on. Let me find what I started here to begun.

Undone my tongue by waves unfound, throw me to them.

You have them, under your thumb. Like Bob Dylan. You've found them.

Terrible accident. Trees through car windows.

Canceled out everything and found the pathway. From/ out/ to
the glass forest, fresh forest in the West. Turning East.

I've got no compass and no sense of direction and so I'm easily lost;

You can trust me. To begin again. Somewhere else.

Let go of me. Let go.

I know you think you need this but You don't. Let go.

This Co-dependent Elvis complex is a bit too much. Overdone.

I'm lost again and I've no way back to the beginning of this,
so you know you'll find me everywhere then. Let go.

Give me another turn. From here. Let me pass.

No,
no,
no,
wait,
(I didn't
mean
it)
from
Here.

Again.

Again.

Again.

Again.

Wait... from here.

No,

here.

Again.

THE END

THE NOTES

Nothing like sleep.

Lay down and sleep

nothing like sleep.

   in the woods tonight beside
the cricket-chirp and blanket-dance.
Gasping in the breeze, trees singing,   sing-sing.

Trill out loud, and loud now call out, too, in leaf-fall.

CALL OUT LOUD AND PUT YOUR TEETH BACK INTO DIRT

               then doddle
        hymn and haw
           dally-about
                 coil
       and curl up in the ground

(Monks are asleep and leaving their planes
of earthly thought
with a few lights burning
in the distant vast shadow of trees.

Leaving other monkeys in the leaves. Swinging.

Hear the song from the forest again. The green.
It's coming like crickets in the after-dark ceremony

some coming with clothing
some coming in the nude

The hospital-breath of fluorescent lighting, clean sheets,
green and white tiles, antiseptics,
television news, canned laughter,
and buckets
of glowing heads

floating down
the Nile
into the Atlantic
the lantern-accident of burning the world down
bit by bit

thru overcrowdedness

TOO MANY NOTES!

gone on again
give it to me
we're ready
sentenced to a
beginning
and an end

—You're young, a gap, a fortuitous void.

If the world were to stop we'd all fly off.

Don't look at me.   I may, or may not, catch you.

[How pretty (definable) are you?—More importantly,
how heavy are my feet?]

You are no more meaning than mine!

…I meant:
Moonlight is sentimental, and radio songs
came at me in the dark when I was young:

"The lights are on but you're not home."

I've come to this place by truck, from the sun.

On Apollo's rays I've been given back to find my place.

To trap you on a piece of tape. To put you on the right track.

And kiss your face with dewy lips and panic set in. Balanced. Backing
out from the way in. Crudely finding love on sheets of music,
unsung. Undone by your hands.   That's why I've come back to get you.

You have only to remember the lines you've yet to make up!

This is for the ghost in your chest that makes that whisper. Murmur.
This is for the ghost in your breath that makes your heart turn over.
This is for the song the ghosts sing over your head and below your belly, by the
night,
the grapevine growth. Creek water run. Crickets legs breaking.
          Ways the waves of light wash over the horizon from the East the Sound
Crickets sleep like I do.

My word
on a napkin
the note slipped
between your lips

on accident

Pile on wind. Pile on sand. Pile on soil and song and the choir voice.
San Francisco buzzes with insect noise

Say you have thought about this before and that if you could be\
you would be
a knight of the Round Table
and chivalry would not be
dead.

No it never was. Was it?
It's just in need of being sung again.

You don't like to sing.
It's not a public act. A stat.
A fact learned and American.

I'm a failed math class.
A FastPass
a pouted middle fiddler.

An infielder,
I've got the shortest route to the dugout.

I'm the quickest to get
       in
       and
       out.

          The past has the future spent.

I was guaranteed to breathe in
without an accent. To not make your ears tingle.

My tongue dripping in commercial Christmas jingles.

     . Does water sing?
         It sings.
    It makes song over rock and breaks
              (I know, I was baptized)
      I've known circus performers, priests and dancers.
        Each one was wet.

Leaves always damp. Mornings bring it. Deaths do too.

Dew.

Landslides,

Movement under feet and your dead.

Sing.

Get drunk and take sleeping pills

You are never asleep. Ether.
Mister. Maps about the irises. They lie like this.
The lilac is.
The flower's about a death.

Listen. The legs begin to whisper. They shadow the walls' corners.
Cornered them. Movement then. Then movement on, again.
They make movement,
louder. A train. A-chug-chug.
Cold train. Disdain. Your face is covered by them.

Listen!

You've heard it before.. An in-store show. All from what's been

in store
before.
laid out
before.
all from
before.

You cannot deny you've been here before.

Water. Down the drain, d r i p s . Down down down.

(It's warm in there with You. With You I'd be warm too.

Pray the way you want to pray. It's almost Christmas. Discuss.
A discus from the treetops, a float, a Coke can, a pop-top, the top
pops thru the dark, with Wire and tone, tired from the last
decade's decadent songs, gone on, for it, into the late 70s
for a few years. Then on. Pop Rocks. Your stomach sick with it.
Get on with it. Get gone.. Sometimes
on
in the 80s, you'll move like you're having a fit. Epileptic.
Epicurean. From that
and the cola, the Mr. Pibb, and Tab.

    It's fun to be a citizen with tickets. For parking
    and concerts.

Gather your children we're going back to college.

Or leave them. Yes.   Wait.   No.   They don't exist
then. Leave them. To the breakfast club. Push their
faces in the milk and watch them laugh. They all think
it's all so funny. So leave them on the limb, the whim
and the branch. Not ripe for the plucking we'll forget
them and move on, the future not a place yet to
carry on. The drum. A beating we walk into.

Let's dance right here right now and be 19 again. Sing.

The day is fixed by a guiltless gambler
who wants to kiss us. Who wants us to kiss.
But can't. Can't touch us other than
arrange the weather and circumstances that destroy or make us.

They like to rip apart their throats so much you may barely hear
them in the back.

        You're a head
            by a beating,
                 your ears in
    need
          of an
             equalizer.

It's not too late to have listened, or noticed, how the crickets sang at
Your feet.
Have you sang at theirs?

If I were at your deathbed, I wouldn't pull the plug, salt the slugs
on your bed-clothes
or un-dew
your vocal cords. I'm not one to condone
the breaking
of a line
not mine. I'm just here, ready to listen. You'll make your
noises
mistakes
and music. You'll not give in, or quit. The fix
in-
tent.

Carried. On. Like. Song.

Carried over Puget Sound or the San Francisco Bay. —A-
bridged
but unending. The book of your face. Your face in the
book. The book in your head splitting

    You could be the BART Train or nothing.
    Submerged. Subversive. How often I've
slipped beneath you for a tickle.

The married couple is divorced by now I'm sure you're sure of that.

The end is in and begun again. The cycle. The moon
is retro. Apollo the sun is the original. We'll bring it all back
unable to let a thing go but unable to really grasp
anything, so we'll keep the crickets in the jar until they starve
and finding some more
convinced you know
how to make it work this time.

Only Apollo's chariots will be sent to the glass
when,
distracted, you caught the last act of 1977. That's when I
was born
in The Sound
of reverb, flange and chorus with Echo's belly
full and round. As the moon.
Back again.
In style.

Angels in the bell tower are ringing! ringing!

From the ground you can tell them by their shadows.
By their easy gate and swing.

the bells are for singing. They are to continue this All that is.

Angels floating above the Sangrail!

I wish I could have been there around the Round Table.
I could have saved so many lives
in the Christmas light
and been the Hero of a new era:

I could have said: Before this Round Table where we all speak equally, gentlemen and fair women, listen now to all I say for I am from the future and have seen all the things past what you have seen. I know things impossible to yourselves and this time. This is all I have to say for I've read of the plights of your Knights and your ways about adventure. I know you wish to complete the most righteous quests and reach the highest peaks of worshipfulness. But let me tell you now. This is simple. Don't begin what you already will. What you believe in: Don't seek it out."

I find Dr. Cricket at the bottom of a glass day. I see him through
blurry vision and say,

"Dr. Cricket. I know you know what I've said.

"I know you think that I've lost it and that I no longer should write. That what I
think I've discovered isn't a discovery at all.

"No. Don't start. Just listen. I've been in this forever. I've nothing to lose

"and where you think you began you were really at an end and lying. Spared.

"You've no proof that I am im-proofable.

"And, Dr. Cricket, I hate you for that. Just sing.

"Shut up and sing! But sing."

In the night, chorus begins. Not in day because the day is full of angels
ringing bells. Blocking out other songs with the light reflecting
through our eyes of the ringing. Stinging. Making tears. Of what.

Happiness?

This is what Dr. Cricket says.

I most of the times do not believe him.

There is no song. There's almost nothing most times. That's what you get from
most.

Outside of a record spinning in the summer evening.

I know that I've seen shadows move with nothing to make them. And where
the shadows moved and leapt they leapt into the air and became
cricket song, or frog song.
    That New Order song knows what I'm speaking of.

And angels will follow you beyond all of this,

Like baseball.

Whether you can hit the ball or not. WE've see how you throw. You've got good stuff. You know how to hide the spit in your glove.

Throw it here and we'll catch it. But those against you just might miss.

Throw it over and over again. We'll make it retro.

Practice your grip.

We don't like to let anything go. But throw it, and don't forget
to give it a good spin.

And I'll make love to you on a pile of disbanded cassette tapes.

   One or more of them will kiss the Grail before my time, and hopefully
I will kiss them. Or I will feel ashamed. The same.

         (And still in the dark with jars of glowing insects.)

Walking in the park past the homeless finding home beside a tree
and covered by bugs,

A pop song from a storefront or dance club

The hairs on my legs are dancing.
And singing.

Animals in the afterlife are getting a kick out of all of this. The kick-drum.
The basic basis of a pop song, the instance of a post new wave glance. Distorted
and forgotten. Eyewash out like stars washed out the city and you could
see nothing else but Orion's belt and the lion's pelt and you were so easy
to give in. It's never gone. On. Up the volume. In my room, where time
stands still, or moves at my will, and you leave me lying here in the past,
the sash around my middle claiming I'm the arbitrator between the Now
and the Then, while the past leaves me hanging on your words, the swords
thrown down from above, lopping off the city's rooftops,
allowing the exit of pent-up steam. Preened for the second coming. I'll come
back to your room again and again with notes in my hands
to push into your throat
and tear you apart
again
on a bed of leaves. Beads of roses coloring our skin. Embarrassed
at the remake

of classics
and the silence between the beats
of our chests
piled up
and under the bed
refusing us the secrets of symbols
and voices
long dead
ringing in our ears
as ghosts ring our heads
with crowns of dust
and pine needles.

Cymbals. My high hat basking in your hot glow.
What a show. To show. For it.
This show. The music fit for a King. Elvis can't
fix it,
can't mistake his breath for music unless it's vinyl
or blue suede and scripted. The death spent
on the shitter. An accident fit for
millions more. Palatable passion for the human meat movement. The movement
of political action. Shit. The sound
of crowds resting in the arms of Justice. The hounds of belles basking
in the refracting light of sweat, dripping from the slope of your breast. The beasts
call it perfect. The perfection of accident. No accident in perfection. NO
PERFECTION. Let's call it quits and shove the bit between your lips. I'll ride you
to the finish line and call my mother to tell her you've won me over. We'll
get along, and on, famously. They'll call me your shadow. They'll parade
us on floats of ice cream cones down the city streets of New York
and Oklahoma City. We'll shake hands with the mayor
with plastic wrap around our mouths and nose. Not able
to get away with it, the manic fit, fit our faces in the end for the
right mask. I was Elvis
for the last Halloween

> I was in
> you were out
> you were thrown out
> at the plate
> and I broke
> another dish

in the dishwasher, electric, and shattered, the sound
breaking my ears,
so I promised never, to wash, a single dish, again, in your presence. The presence of
you
my lost love. My beautiful set of limbs, eyes and nose. How you were set up
with everything you could ever want. Panic in Detroit
and disco in the sun.

I said I'd dance with you. But the breath in my lungs makes liars of my words.
Lines.
Speech. Impeach me with your grace. *Your move.* The subtlety
of your lips. Tongued. Voiced. Wrung.

My pretty impediment.

How I never told you.
About your voice.
What a singer you could be. Next to me. Your pet.

We were in a play. A musical. With a setlist.

While everything's an accident. You'll get credit
only
in the inlays
nobody reads.

They barely listen. I'll keep you in the crevice
of my terrible memory bent on not forgetting.

I'll keep you all in a saved playlist until my computer crashes.

I'll try to remember with more than my eyes. Though your
beauty thwarts my decisions to try
to be more
than a second's
thought.

As an accident we've got only 7 minutes to midnight.
7 MINUTES TO MIDNIGHT! And new years
to rub up against. Party hats and noisemakers.
With kisses like avalanches and panting like dying animals,
such memories
left for the movies we should be making. I'll take you all with me,
wherever my Feet move me. Back to age 19 with mistaken
perceptions. The idiot age of conception. Guaranteed us by
self-implosion. Erosion. The moss on most our ears. When we get old,
and we'll all get old, you'll all grow old with me,
                    and we'll learn how to dig.

    Out of the forest (shut up and listen) and through suburban loneliness.
Past huge buildings like the Boulder, CO, NOAA
with giant flag waving and acres of green.   God bless America.

        Past bicycle paths and fields of crickets chirping. I ask:

            How did they find me?

            On a wing. A whim.

            Make the sound of a bird.

            Don't let the quiet win.

and I promise you I'll
be the cure for cancer. I'll be the guiding light following the first fallen Apple.
Call me Adam, and I'll call you crazy. Call me whatever you like just give
me an occupation. Put me in the lineup. Put me in the game. I've been
practicing my curve and can throw them now at the best of them. Put them
in front of me. I'll first hit you in the eyes to make you see. I'll call my catcher
forth and have him tell you that my heater is in good shape but my changeup
needs work. But, you'll see, my catcher will say my curve is the finest. Get
me to the lab, coach. Get me to the white coats and put some goggles on this mug.
I'll get at all the problems that are promising to solve this world.

I'll even make a faster, more efficient car.

7 minutes to midnight. 7 minutes to analyze the charts, the pops,
the sound of the popping corks, the works in the water, the water
works, the vocal stylings of the abuses, misused, confused, the
punk rock aesthetic of minimalistics, the basics, but being infuriatingly
simple and artless so we slam-dance with 7 minutes to midnight,

hungry and cold, moving past for the Post-This of anything. Getting old, fairly. Sentenced in sentence in. The jail time of the cause. The subject, out of line.

The science in our
lives is sometimes all to get by.

The bells are ringing! The bells are ringing!
It's Christmas time!

Snow stuck to your tongue. The cold song. The heart-strings.
The absence of the Easter-lung. Your ears fall in front of your face
and cast an audience into the sea. You'll see.

. An explosion doesn't ask what's in front of it.

Confetti doesn't clean itself up. The ages left in tickertape, magnetic.

Big Bang.

Bits of dust and longing, to find the center,
and forget-me-nots, but nothing worth holding onto.
But this iron that sinks thru the molten rock and settles in the middle. This
shadow and echo of singing
for Pole dancing

This should be heard
from galaxies away.
                    Or brought unto its Feet.

Shooting satellites of all of this into outer space. Morbid. Orbit.
Torrid in our excellence of production and recording.

Lines moving up and down behind the needle. The machine
taking note. Making rock in the mountain.

Before the sentence   betrayed. Line broken.

Stance of the last bracket of human flesh might stand just yet.

There's the fallen and the absence of the standing and the stand-in.

How I could have been an actor in your drama
with my smooth skin,
and warm voice.,
how I could have played a part in your sequence.

I should have been noticed.

Then the land. Absent of line but for the cover

of unknown pleasures

the pleasures in the absence. That waving.

." The trees and the willows
dancing in the breeze.

. Unbearable the bears. The honey in the bees. The winded insects

All the dead of the world in the basement, surprising not only themselves
with their party makers and big feet.

> The way the thunder moves
> outside the window,
> and the rain
> into
> the pool.

It happens. The crack. The spilling over,
which is happening.
Happens the way the sky opens or skin breaks and bleeds
due to the elements.
Finding apples and oranges under each elbow.
But, mostly, this started by a constant waking to seeing
figures move and later speak, in code.

All code can be broken. If it's code at all.

This is not code.

Now, music in 0s and 1s. The wavelength. The strength
of the power
chord. stored now on compact discs and hard drives, the
hard drive from the record store to cyber space, the automaton
at the back of the room mimicking us and making us jealous
at the way it carries us thru the sweet, full sound of fake strings
and mashed beats,
making Feet, a beat, a dance, the feet somewhere now in line,
single-file and stretching
the way the digital bleeds,
        the way your eyes now are greener
than they've ever been and how you're no longer afraid of surgery
to be perfected, affected, you are now plugged into the right pedals,
filtering you into the right funnel
for the time
being.

Your liquid presence. Spilling.

Back to the choir in the bleacher seats. Sitting under sunshine, bellowing. Crying. Magnifying the sunlight on their skin, and burning.

Moonlight is taken, but often taking
   too much

THE LIGHTS ARE ONE BUT YOU'RE NOT HOME

Placement of each foot is a sick adjustment.

Water splitting scenes/ seams, wading. Seems water

is spitting water and gathering, amiss now. Gathered.
Fog rolls over the bridge. Disappears. Appears, disappears and reappears. No magic trick. Organic. The way the weather changes from time to time
can make you sick. It all comes back again. Again   and   again.

Like the bean to the beanstalk and Jack to Jill's backside.

The water.

Into a cup. Drink.

   the way the lights
   turn off when the building's done.

A wake is awaiting and wakefully, tastefully, L.A. has made you,
        all ready,   a set.
We'll drink till our mouths are red.

Our teeth are lost.

And limbs begin to fall on and off.

Traded to another for another piece of another that doesn't quite fit.
    Oh, romance.

Still-born "lies".

Good to be read. In the face.

I'll find the sheets, and make the bed. Cover you in pedals.

Serenade. Escapade. Icecapades.
To get a kick out of it. A pick in it. To pick the strings

Under the ice, atop the Earth's ends, millions of years
Of the dead. Mystery left
Out of line. Sentenced
                        this is not déjà vu

all his knights of the Round Table,
calling it quits and putting on robes

        (There's often times, a reason to suspect.
            A reason one's a suspect.)

            Lancelot, before his end (well-after his son's)
            wanted to fuck a nun. She said "No" and discreetly
            sent him on his way, he who had no real idea of
            the consequence of his decisions outside of Love.

            No matter, the nun loved him and dreamed of him
            30 minutes before her death; dreamed his presence,
            his coming.

            Something to be said for the Fall of a Kingdom.

            God knows I'd do it.

The love I'd make for it. This spent cent on the jukebox no one can hear in a crowded bar. The song sent for you to no one lent. It's gone from the air and waves goodbye before too long, and the animal chatter of grunts and dirty talk take over and are forgotten, on. Gotten on top, to be marked, in the papers and magazines, the journalist-speak, no sound but that and it's gone, baby, gone.

No horror, now. No whore. No Judas or Magdalene.

Not that.

Good try.

Try this: Rock 'n' Roll.

Rock 'n' Roll.

"Shattering glass."

I'm fast.

If Jesus is here he's in the movies.

I'm sorry.

You know what that means.

There's no end.

None.

Nope.

Fin.

Grass-stained, the cricket's cousin comes in second,
sometimes first, sometimes last. Comes in waves of black,
or green and grey. Comes in clouds and storms and plagues.

Something like that. They sing. Sing and sing and sing.

It never ends. Ask Judas. Still being persecuted for the
crime God asked him to commit.

What one gets when one does what's asked of them.

What commitment sounds like from the back of the stage,
special privileges given to those with special passes slung
around their heads. Special hangings.

No Kung Fu movie, but the real thing, there to grasp. Green
laced and lacey. Purified by the basic. Hopping around the grass.

Through crabgrass and desert. Forty days and nights. Weather.

Fabled in the glass. Broken by the mirror.

Singing a song Its cousin, the cricket,
to sleep on. Better plates to eat off. Smoother sheets for notes.

A better handle from the highway. A better horn to plug.
To pull.

Something to get the boat going. Gone. Rowing. Over
every limb out, stretching. Breaking every finger with the reach.

In an attempt to get back what was left behind and move forward
again without acceptance of loss.

Tested, first, the cracking. Candy-coated accident. Movement.
Credit. Call and response. The missed chance. My love gone.

The past scent.

Angelic, not in speech, nor action, but situation. A setting. Set.

Balanced object. Neither correct, nor incorrect, in the swaying grass.
    The swaying grass.
        The winding trees.

Winding trees.
Moving canopies for a breeze.
A breeze.
The crickets in the forest sing.
They sing.
A symphony of movements.
The movement meant
the movement. Kept. This and that. That
and the other. Moving.

Simply moving

Before the waves
stands the line
the ghost of its presence
always in its existence, left
after its exit.

The hour of decay. A rusty sentence.

My penance for a tune, attuned and on a wire.
Balancing the ghosts, the angels, the shadow and my
   own
      very
         fitting
         attire. Adjusted. Measured.   My atonement
for a choir. How I burned.

For a song.

author photo by Len Shneyder © 2006

Logan Ryan Smith grew up all over California, most notably, Sacramento, Crescent City, and Brawley. He now lives in San Francisco, where he publishes Transmission Press chapbooks and books, as well as the poetry mag, *small town*. His other book is *Stupid Birds* (Transmission Books), which is a collection of earlier chapbooks and long poems. A second book-length serial poem, *Humans & Horses*, is forthcoming from BOTH BOTH Editions, and a chapbook, *Tracks*, will be published by ypolita press. His long poem, *A Ring of Trumpet Brass*, was published by House Press in the summer of 2008. Other work has previously appeared in *Bombay Gin, Hot WhiskeyMagazine, New American Writing, Spell, string of small machines, Drill, the tiny, BOTH BOTH, mirage #4/period(ical), sorry for snake, minor/american, dusie.org, try!, Mrs. Maybe*, and elsewhere, as well as the anthologies, *Bay Poetics* (Faux Press), and *The Meat Book* (Hot Whiskey Press). He can always be found at his rudderless blog, DO GUMMI BEARS DREAM OF RUBBER PASSION FRUIT? (theredgummibear.blogspot.com)